Inspired
Every Day

Inspired
Every Day

*Essays and Stories to Brighten Your Day,
Give You Hope, and Strengthen Your Faith*

Patricia Crisafulli

Copyright © 2013 by Patricia Crisafulli
Cover image by Pat Commins; design by Neil A. Heacox

978-1-4976-4954-5

Distributed in 2014 by Open Road Distribution
345 Hudson Street
New York, NY 10014
www.openroadmedia.com

Dedicated to my sisters, Jeanine and Bernadette, with love.

Table of Contents

TABLE OF CONTENTS

Foreword

Stories that Inspire . . . Every Day

We are a people of stories. Sacred texts, collective histories, and literature tell us who we are. Stories chronicle life as we experience it and understand it to be. No matter how unique the individuals, stories at their very essence are universal. Anyone who has told a story—even a simple anecdote—and heard the response, "The same thing happened to me!" has witnessed the connection that is possible through stories.

Whether they are fiction or nonfiction, whether populated with imaginary characters or drawn from our own lives, stories speak truth. Stories offer a vision of what is possible—the love, healing, and grace that are available in abundance, just for the asking. Stories inspire faith and celebrate hope.

Faith is the consoling truth that something beyond ourselves is accessible and available and waiting to partner with us. Whatever one's own interpretation, inwardly, faith encompasses one's beliefs and, outwardly, it colors experiences and expression in the world. With faith, we can see little miracles everywhere—the signposts on the path and the affirmation that we're not alone.

Hope is faith's companion, the encouragement to keep on the journey. Faith sees the new possibilities and hope takes us to them. Faith considers different outcomes than what has limited us before, and hope finds a way to pursue them. Hope is stirring and compelling, and it can overcome fear, indifference, and a lack of momentum. Hope says keep going—there is much in you that needs to be expressed.

With faith and hope, we can move a mountain, or at least dislodge the stone that resides within, the one that blocks us from experiencing the fullness of who we were created to be. We tune out the discouragement of the world with all its negativity and "no," and acknowledge the directive that we were *all* given: to tell and share our wisdom and what we've come to know. The way we do that is with our stories.

Inspired Every Day is a collection of stories, both fiction and nonfiction. Whether made up or personal experiences, these stories celebrate and honor reconnection, possibility, forgiveness, family, love, joy—and finding moments of extraordinary grace in the midst of ordinary life.

Patricia Crisafulli

Inspired
Every Day

Holding On to a Strong Hand

An Essay

Answers to prayers come in a variety of forms, whether as the long-awaited positive outcome or as the strength to endure a negative turn of events. Hope and encouragement are whispered in holy words or shouted in mundane ones heard on the radio. Inspiration never ceases its communication.

And so it was for me while I prayed for guidance, discerning where my path lay. But as I looked for knowledge and assurance of where I needed to go next, the answers seemed to elude me. Like most situations, the particular circumstance on my mind was complicated by layers and nuances; I needed to tread lightly and cautiously. Even this fool didn't dare rush in.

Day after day, I prayed for direction; even a hint or a clue would suffice. Then one day, when I stopped asking the questions long enough to become attuned to the answers, an image came to mind. In it, a little girl in a dark blue dress coat and matching hat was being held tightly by the hand as her mother guided her through the maze of a crowd. Perhaps it was a busy department store or a train station at rush hour. Wherever they were, the place was so thick with people dashing about, that a child of six or seven could be easily lost, if not for the strong hand of her mother.

As I contemplated the image, I knew that the little girl didn't need to know where they were headed, whether up the stairs or the escalator, or down a long hallway. It didn't matter if they were taking a shortcut because they were pressed for time, or the longer way around because it would be less crowded. She only needed to feel the firm grip of a loving, assured hand.

This mental picture, assembled from whatever "clip art" I carried in my subconscious, brought me great comfort. No, I do not have the definitive answers to my lingering questions. I cannot tell you that my path is now well-defined or more clearly marked.

All I know is I have the confidence and comfort of that little girl, with a Loving Parent who holds me firmly by the hand and steers me along, step for step. I cannot get lost and, ultimately, I will get to where I am supposed to go (or in the least, I will get somewhere)—provided I never let go of that Hand.

Why Geese Don't Fly

A Story

Joshua hurled a small stone with pinpoint accuracy, hitting the goose in the middle of its thick body and sending it skyward in a flurry of beating wings and splashing water. Hoping no one had seen what he'd done, Joshua got back on his bike and pedaled as fast as he could out of the park, away from the pond, away from the geese and, if his legs could have taken him that far, away from the town he didn't want to live in.

Unlocking the back door, Joshua entered the quiet

house. He remembered California again, coming home from school on fall days, knowing his mother would be there and working in her studio. Sometimes she'd sit at the counter, sipping green tea for the antioxidants that would keep her from getting cancer. Green tea didn't prevent getting hit by a drunk driver.

Joshua hated Wisconsin *and* the fact that they had moved because their grandfather lived there. At 14, he didn't need anybody while his father was at work or traveled for business, not like his sister, Cindy, who was only 7. As soon as he graduated from high school in four years, he was out of there.

His solitude was broken by the rumble of the school bus, and he hurried out the door to meet Cindy on the corner. By the time he got back to the house, his grandfather was pulling in the driveway. Joshua turned away, just as his grandfather asked him a question, "You wanna come to Best Buy with me later?" Joshua told him he had a lot of homework, but his grandfather insisted, saying he'd pick him up at 7:30.

The store was cavernous as a warehouse and brightly lit. Joshua wandered over to the videogames for a while. When he went back, his grandfather had found a laptop that seemed like a pretty good deal.

On the way home, his grandfather tried to make conversation but Joshua only stared out the window into the nothingness beyond the intermittent glow of a few street-lights. Then his grandfather made an unexpected right turn down a road that ended with a crunch of gravel at the edge of a marsh.

Joshua spoke up, but his grandfather shushed him and, opening the car door quietly, motioned for him to follow. Deep into the cattails, the water oozing up from beneath their feet, they crouched low. "Just listen," the old man whispered.

Above the crackling of the wind in the cattails and creak of tree branches, they heard the low honking of geese. As time passed and more flocks landed in the swamp, Joshua forgot the scene in the park earlier that day and just lis-tened to the voices of the birds, thinking that if his mother could see him now, she'd be proud of him for being there with his grandfather, watching the geese settle in for the night. He could picture her, smiling at him over her mug of green tea, and telling him to take it easy on his grand-father, that he was only trying to help. After a while, they walked in silence back to the car.

"I love to listen to them fly in at night," his grandfather explained as they drove back home. "This is their staging area, where they come for food, water, and rest before taking off again."

"So why don't they all go?" Joshua asked. "The geese at the park don't seem to be going anywhere."

His grandfather said he didn't know, but maybe they could find out.

Two days later, when he turned on his computer, Joshua was surprised to find three e-mails in the inbox, all from his grandfather. The first was to say hi, the second to say he could email back any time, and the third to say he figured out why some geese don't fly away.

Joshua started to delete the emails, disappointed that they weren't from his friends in California, but thinking of what his mother would have said to him, he wrote back instead. *Good job on the email. So what's up with the geese?* The next day an explanation awaited him:

> *Lots of theories on the geese. People used to raise decoy geese to attract wild ones for hunting (which sounds pretty dumb to me). They think a lot of these geese are decoys gone wild. And some people say the geese just like it here. Too bad it's not mutual. Too much goose poop in the park for some folks. But if I were a goose, I'd stay here, too.*

Joshua typed a quick reply. *That's cool about the geese. Who cares about the goose poop. Poop happens, right? LOL.*

The reply was nearly instantaneous with a question

about who "LOL" was, and then Joshua's explanation about "laugh out loud." He signed it *See ya later, Grand-Dude.*

LOL. That's a good one. Glad you like the geese. Maybe you'll stay or maybe you'll migrate one day.

But for now, I'm glad you're here. Love ya, Grand-Dude.

The Women Who
Came Before Me

An Essay

The moment has come for me, as it does for so many adult daughters, when the face in the mirror is no longer my own. There is my mother, looking back at me.

My resemblance to her is strong—the same deep-set dark eyes, the wide smile. Yet, beyond facial shape and expression there is an even deeper link, more powerful than any genetic code. There's our family tree, our shared history. Indeed, the person looking back in the mirror is an amalgam of many others.

The legacy of inheritance, admittedly both positive and

negative, can be claimed with a shift in perspective. The woman I resemble, the one who nurtured me and my two sisters, was not just "mother." She was also *the woman who came before me.*

From this perspective, I gain deeper insights into my mother, who died twenty-seven years ago when I was 26. I see her in the light of her multiple roles: wife, mother, sister, friend, and as a woman in historical context—a child of the Depression, a bride in the years following World War II, and a traditionalist during the rebellious 1960s.

Seeing my mother as a woman from a certain time and place, I understand our differences in opinion (she saw women as living in a "man's world," which I refused to accept). Even more important, I appreciate her as a woman making her way in the world. Although she was a small-town housewife, she was keenly interested in other cultures, and even traveled to Peru with one of my sisters because she longed to see firsthand the ruins of an ancient civilization. Her book collection was not only Betty Crocker but also explorer Roy Chapman Andrews. Returning as I have just recently from yet another trip to Africa, I believe my mother would be proud of my adventurousness and revel in every tale.

In the mirror of my life, I see traces of other generations—grandmothers who had strong traits of resilience and resourcefulness. My maternal grandmother, who came to the United States from France after World War I with her new American husband, helped keep the family farm during the Depression by making wreaths. She'd sit up half the night, weaving ground pine over willow frames until her hands bled. In the morning, my grandfather would catch the milk train to Syracuse, where he sold those wreaths door to door.

Other women, too, make up this chain: aunts who by day cleaned house, planted gardens, made meals, and did laundry. But when they dressed up for special occasions they, like Mom, transformed themselves with their high heels and chic dresses. They will forever define "glamour" for me.

In the face in the mirror, I see them all. But my appreciation is clearest when I put down the lens of being the daughter, granddaughter, or niece. Moving beyond those roles, I truly come to understand them all as the women who came before me.

Sweet as a Peach

A Story

The day bloomed warm under a sun that had been hesitant all spring to show its strength until finally coaxed out into fullness as May became June. Tempted by the sun and the breeze off the lake, Virginia passed her usual bus stop on the way home from work and kept walking. Today, the streets of Chicago seemed as exotic to her as a piazza in Italy or a boulevard in Paris. Forty-five minutes later and three blocks from the building where she lived, she stopped at a Thai restaurant and asked for an order of Siam chicken with cashews to go. At the next block, a scrap of opera caught her ear. Giovanni, the green grocer who owned the corner store, blasted the music through the open door. As Virginia approached, she heard him singing along, quite badly.

"Buena sera!" she called out. Giovanni answered with a litany of musical-sounding, incomprehensible Italian.

Virginia stopped to pick out a small plastic container of pineapple, three apples, and two ripe bananas.

Giovanni pawed through a display of peaches, selecting a perfect rosy-gold orb and offered it to her. "This is no ordinary peach. Oh, no!" He wagged his finger. "It will bring true love and happiness—happiness as sweet as this peach. My treat!"

Virginia laughed and bade him good night.

The next morning, she put the peach in a bag with her lunch and set off for work. At midmorning, the chime on her computer sounded with the arrival of an email: her friends, Dolores and Rick, were having an impromptu dinner party on Saturday evening.

Virginia's fingers hovered over the keyboard, ready to decline—dinner parties meant being the odd chair at a table set for couples. Besides, she had a million things to do on Saturday.

Like what? The ferocity of that thought slapped away

her hands from the decline she was about to type. Virginia hit send, accepting the invitation before she could change her mind.

The skirt swished around her knees, a bright collage of turquoise, yellow, and rose with tiny opalescent sequins that caught the light and yet were subtle enough not to be flashy. She wore a turquoise top that the woman at the store had said was perfect, even though Virginia thought it was too young for her, with its hint of a cap sleeve and wide, open neckline. She added a gold rope necklace bought in Italy years ago and a pair of dangling earrings. Virginia checked her appearance in the mirror one more time and left before she had time to change her mind and put on something more sensible.

Arriving at the dinner party, Virginia accepted hugs from Dolores and compliments on her outfit. After offering to help, Virginia took a plate of appetizers out to the patio where other guests mingled. A short while later, Dolores introduced a man who'd just arrived. "Friends, this is Stuart," Dolores announced. "He's a consultant who works with Rick. You've been here, what, two months?"

"Three months yesterday," Stuart replied, his accent

hitting Virginia's ears like an old song she hadn't heard in years.

As cocktails moved to dinner, Virginia found a place at a table set with an even number of chairs. "Do you mind?" Stuart asked, sliding out the chair beside her.

"Not at all." She imagined how he might feel in a room of people he didn't know. "So what brings you here from England?"

Stuart's eyes crinkled. "That accent of mine gives me away, doesn't it?" His story came out in conversation, including the latest installment of moving to Chicago from Atlanta after his wife died four years earlier. His smile had the softness of old sadness worn smooth.

When Stuart asked about her life, Virginia wasn't sure what to say. "I like to travel, although it's been many years since my last big trip." The festiveness of the evening made her bold. "If I could go anywhere, it would be Egypt. I watched a documentary on ancient Alexandria last night."

"Me, too!" Stuart exclaimed. "Oh, I'd go in a minute." Virginia laughed. "I probably won't get farther than the Field Museum."

"Do they have an Egypt exhibit?" Stuart asked. "Shall we find out?"

As she and Stuart talked like old friends and not new acquaintances, Virginia caught Dolores's glance across the table and the smile in her eyes. When dessert was served—peach shortcake with whipped cream—Virginia nearly laughed aloud as she recalled Giovanni's gift and his prediction of happiness. Ignoring the calories, she savored the first bite.

Later that evening, as they all returned to the patio, Virginia took a seat beside Stuart and looked up into the evening sky. Gazing at the shining quarter moon, Virginia decided it was a luscious evening—the fresh ripeness of early summer now unfolding new possibilities, which made life sweet—indeed, as sweet as a peach.

A Fortune of Wisdom
in a Ten-dollar Bill

An Essay

No matter how much money has come and gone through my fingers in the sixteen years since it happened, I have never forgotten this particular ten-dollar bill—the one I never received from the ATM and then got back with life-changing abundance.

It was late on a Thursday afternoon, just a few minutes after five o'clock, and I had stopped at the ATM at my local bank branch between coming home from work and picking up my then 4-year-old son from preschool. I punched in the numbers and out came two twenties and a receipt for a fifty-dollar withdrawal. No ten-dollar bill.

Of course the bank was closed. And of course there was no one to call and complain. Feeling robbed, cheated, unfairly treated, I indulged in self-righteous victimhood all the way to the preschool parking lot.

The next day, I couldn't get that lost ten-dollar bill out of my mind. I tried rationalizing—surely I'd spent far larger amounts on foolish things. I told myself the least I could do was let the bank know there was something wrong with the ten-dollar-bill dispenser on the machine. I wasn't expecting any restitution, but maybe it would constitute a good deed (and I could have the satisfaction of complaining).

I arrived ten minutes earlier this time, at five minutes before five. Since it was Friday, the bank was open late. The place was packed, with a long line in front of the tellers. I told myself I should just leave; I was wasting my time on a fool's errand with nothing to be gained. Besides, my son was waiting for me at preschool.

That's when I noticed a young woman looking anxiously toward the tellers. When we made eye contact, she told me her "problem." She had come to the bank the day before when it was closed and the ATM gave her too much money—an extra ten dollars. One minute separated the time stamp on her receipt and mine.

"I don't want to take what's not mine," the young woman said haltingly, her speech and mannerisms indicating a developmental disability. "It's not mine. I don't want the ten dollars. I came to give it back."

A banker stopped to ask if she could help us, and I explained the situation. The young woman piped up: "I don't want this ten dollars. It doesn't belong to me."

"What are the chances," the banker said softly as she examined our receipts.

Such a coincidence had divine fingerprints all over it, a teaching moment if I were willing to learn the lesson.

I asked the banker for two fives. "This ten dollars belongs to both of us," I told the young woman. "You have half and I have half." She beamed as she put the money in her pocket.

I left the bank with five dollars, not ten, and a fortune in wisdom. What's truly mine can never be taken away from me, and sometimes the real blessing is in what I have to share.

The Days of Magical Thinking

A Story

On a warm spring evening in mid-May, Marjorie Leigh Connors drove out of her way with her 6-year-old daughter in the backseat to find a rabbit. She absolutely, positively could not go home until she spied one of the rodents, which had always seemed abundant in their neighborhood—especially the year before when she'd bought an organic repellent made from coyote urine to keep them out of her garden. Now she sought them, welcomed them, as if her daughter's life depended on it.

At block eleven or twelve, a rabbit loped across the

pavement and into a yard where it stopped and looked at her. "Do you see him, Bunny?" Marjorie stopped in the middle of the street, ignoring the car behind them. The driver blared the horn, startling the rabbit; it retreated toward the shrubbery. Marjorie waved in the rearview mirror as she accelerated again, too happy to be annoyed. Her daughter, Beatrice "Bunny" Connors, was going to live; she just knew it.

They'd named her Beatrice for Roger's grandmother, a stately old English woman who lived in Cornwall, whom Marjorie had met just once when she and Roger traveled to England after they became engaged to meet his extended family. Three years later, Grandma Beatrice died in her sleep, and two years after that, their baby girl came into the world. Marjorie suggested the name, which she loved because of the association with the old woman who had instantly welcomed her into the family and for the solid old-fashioned sound of it. On a playground full of Madisons and Brittanys, there wouldn't be another Beatrice.

On their daughter's first birthday, Roger brought home a collector's edition of Beatrix Potter's books, with whimsical drawings of Peter Rabbit, Tom Kitten, and Jemima Puddle-Duck. "You're my bunny," Marjorie had breathed into the soft hair, drinking in that sweet baby smell. The name stuck; by the time she could talk, even Beatrice called herself Bunny.

Roger's car was already in the garage when Marjorie pulled in the driveway. "There's my girl." Roger opened his arms and scooped Bunny up in a hug. "How was the doctor's?"

Bunny showed him the Band-Aid covering the spot where blood had been drawn from her arm and then announced that they'd seen a rabbit. "Really? At the doctor's office?"

"No, driving. Mommy took me to see one."

Roger set Bunny down but kept a hand on her shoulder. "I know you have your superstitions and talismans, or whatever they are, but don't do this to her."

"I'm not doing anything *to* her," Marjorie snapped, grabbing her purse and keys from the table. "We saw a rabbit on the way home. Period." She left without saying where she was going, and came back an hour later with grocery bags.

Roger met her at the back door, not with a hug or apology, which she would have accepted, but with admonishment for departing the way she had and upsetting Bunny. "She needs both her parents—calm and rational." His emphasis on the last word hit her.

PATRICIA CRISAFULLI

"I am rational, but I'm also emotional—and emotional beings need something to hang on to besides science." Marjorie slammed the bag with the organic produce—fresh, raw, healthy as the rabbits ate—on the counter.

"Then go to church or light a candle or something. But this rabbit stuff . . ." Roger shook his head.

To cut the tension at dinner that evening, they both focused their attention on Bunny. That night, Marjorie curled her body away from Roger, refusing to acknowledge the light touch on her back. "You don't understand me," she accused him.

"I don't understand anything—none of this at all." After a while, she succumbed to the arm around her waist and fell asleep.

Brushwood Children's Hospital was rated one of the best pediatric cancer treatment centers in the country, three years running. If Roger wanted empirical evidence, Marjorie thought, there it was. She looked away when the nurse started the first IV and then turned back with a smile. Bunny's eyes traced the long tubing all the way up to the bag on the steel pole.

Another nurse came in a little while later, asking Bunny if she wanted a blanket. When the little girl nodded, the nurse spread a green-and-white checked flannel cover across the bed.

Marjorie leaned in closer. On each check of the blanket was a tiny rabbit sitting high on haunches, resting on all fours, arched in mid-hop, or springing into the air. A laugh escaped in a large gasp, with a wave of tears behind it.

"There's your proof," Roger told her with a firm arm around her shoulders. "More rabbits than you ever chased out of the garden."

"You don't believe that." Marjorie reached for a tissue to blot her eyes.

"If rabbits make you feel better and more positive and that makes Bunny calmer and happier, then I do believe it."

They began counting them, naming them, and claiming each of them as their own, their friend, and something tangible to cling to, as an IV dripped its magic fluid into Bunny's arm.

In Praise of My Imperfect Garden

An Essay

Mother Nature can be quite the tempest.

An infestation of beetles left the roses a little ragged. Slugs or bugs perforated the sweet potato vines cascading from the twin planters by the front door. Blistering sun parched the pansies. As if to add further injury to all that insult, wind gusts from a sudden rainstorm snapped off two pink-and-white starburst lilies I had planted just the day before.

Gardens, however, grow in spite of various strains of pestilence, from blights that turn green leaves into a mot-

tled yellow and brown to voracious insects with an appe-
tite for whatever it is you're growing. Even when things
go right, what passes for perfection fades all too quickly.
A rosebud that unfolds with rows of petals like ruffles on a
bridal gown will only look like that for a day, maybe two.
The margin between bloom and overblown is very narrow.

Gardens, like life, are never without problems. Show
me perfection in either place and I'll show you plastic. All
living things face their challenges; there is no growth without some grief. Instead of going with the flow—deciding that this is a good year for petunias but the geraniums
couldn't keep up—we struggle to compartmentalize
our joy here and disappointment there. Our judgments
become binary: all good or all bad. Yet even amid the
flawed, there is beauty and resilience.

The rosebushes that received only the teeniest bit of
anti-bug spray survived the infestation and kept blooming.
Sure, they lost half their blossoms, but that didn't deter
them from putting forth more buds. In fact, snipping off
the damage seemed to stimulate more growth. As for the
decorative sweet potato vines with Swiss cheese leaves in
places, a good trim tidied them up. Then, sure enough,
new tendrils soon replaced the ravaged foliage.

The life lesson here is obvious but bears a moment of
contemplation. Even when there are problems, there is

some joy to be found somewhere, often in several places. Our worried eyes may focus on life's equivalent of lost leaves and damaged blossoms, but that's not all there is to see, as I discovered one day.

Butterfly bushes planted on either side of the front entrance use their purple-coned flowers to emit a heady perfume and attract visitors. Amber-winged butterflies with a span the size of my palm sip nectar before floating off on the slightest breeze. Others, blue-black with white spots, move their perfectly symmetrical wings in a slow ballet. Then there was a black one with orange-red markings that lit on the uppermost blossom, just a foot in front of me. Its left wing was perfect; the right was missing a lower lobe, torn off like a corner of scrap paper.

How could a delicate thing survive such damage, I thought, convinced that it could not fly. I waited, afraid to watch in case it took a nosedive into the front step. Instead, it lifted off gently into the air and flew across the garden: beautiful imperfection in flight.

Winter Tracks

A Story

They trudged across the snowy field, Robbie in front, followed by Beth, with Susie trailing behind trying to walk
in their footsteps. A snowy Saturday in January had given
them all cabin fever, and raucous play had turned into
bickering. Then Susie started to cry so their mother had
sent them outdoors to play, which for any kid in the 1970s
was hardly punishment.

The siblings set off exploring, over fences and stone
walls and across other people's property. Snow covered
the high grass in the neighbor's lot, turning the scraggly

bushes that grew wild into white lumps. They started to go near the bent stalks of cattails angled out of the snow like giant grasshopper legs.

"Don't go over there," Robbie scolded, pointing to the marshy patch.

Susie pouted, wishing he wouldn't treat her like a know-nothing baby, but followed his tracks more closely. Then Robbie and Beth took off, racing each other to see who could run faster in the deep snow. Being only 7 to Robbie's 12 and Beth's 10, Susie just stood in her tracks, watching them get farther and farther ahead, her nose turning red from the cold and her eyes welling up with tears because she had once again been left behind.

"You're going too fast," Susie whined into the wind that carried her words toward them. "I'll tell Mom!"

"Go on home, Tattletale," Robbie shouted back. The older children stopped and waited for Susie as she trudged ahead. "Try to keep up," Beth told her. "Once we get into the woods, the snow won't be so bad."

"Where are we going?" Susie wiped her nose against her jacket sleeve.

"The rabbit run," Robbie said, without further explanation. "You sure you can make it?"

Susie pulled her wool hat down another half inch over her ears. "Yup."

The rabbit run was a mythical place. Robbie and Beth had stumbled across it the previous winter and had told Susie about it, but she'd been too little to make the trek. Now her curiosity gave her courage.

In winter, as hard as it was to walk, the snow at least kept the wild brambles and thorns at bay. Nature let down those defenses because the cold and ice made a formidable barrier. But not for three hardy country children—or at least two brave ones and one who promised not to cry.

Over the next stone wall, the evergreen trees grew tall and thick and nearly impenetrable. The children had to crawl under the bottom branches, across a carpet of dried fallen needles where only a dusting of snow could reach the ground. Finding a small gap in the trees, they crouched together. The wind rustled—a swirling, hissing sound. They did not speak for fear of breaking the spell.

With a look and a nod, they set off again on their hands and knees under the branches until they reached the edge of a larger clearing ringed by pines on all sides. Why the trees had been cleared in this one spot, they couldn't say. All they knew was the place was special.

Rabbit tracks crisscrossed the clearing, a pattern that spoke of frolicking play, not the race of death from a predator. The tracks doubled-back and looped, circling the base of a few tiny trees that had started to grow in the clearing. The scampering of a field mouse—four tiny paws and the impression left by a nose—made delicate etchings in the snow.

They backed away from the clearing, not wanting to mix their footprints with the animal tracks. It was enough to find this place, to see it with their eyes and imprint it in their memories as undeniable proof that would last well into adulthood and the stories they would tell to their own children one day: that animals play as humans do, racing each other in the snow, moving for the pure joy of it and leaving tracks in the snow.

Dreaming Ourselves into Being

An Essay

As children, we dreamed of what we might become when we grew up—ballerinas and astronauts, movie stars and racecar drivers, and then professions that became more appealing (and realistic) because of our interests, talents, and passions. Some of us stayed true to those plans; others made course corrections or were sidetracked along the way.

Now we are those "grownups," with lives that reflect the sum total of our choices. And yet, we are not done; we are still a work in progress. Just as when we were children, we must dream of what we will become.

When I was 12, I decided to become a writer, and certainly that pursuit has not been as easy as declaring it to be so. But because my "younger self" had the courage to start out on this path, I am writing these words today. As I look ahead today, I once again consider the possibilities for my future. I imagine myself three decades from now, a spry octogenarian who has enjoyed a full life, having written many books (most definitely a novel or two) and who has chronicled her fascinating travels. She has taught writing workshops and encourages others to claim their right to self-expression. Hers has been and continues to be a life of creative purpose.

My "older self" is my North Star. With her in mind, I navigate the course of my life choices that I hope will bring me closer to fulfilling this vision in the future. Of course, there is no guarantee of how things will turn out, but I believe my intentions will be the tipping point toward realization—just as when I was 12 and dreamed of becoming a writer.

With my older self in mind, it was easy to decide last year to start graduate school at the age of 52 to pursue a master's degree in creative writing. How else could she accomplish what I dream for her to do? For her sake, and mine, I vow not to become complacent, whether on creative pursuits or self-care. If I want my older self to look back on her life with joy and gratitude, I must live the life she will want to remember.

So it is with all of us. As we dream ourselves into being, we declare our right to a second half that rivals (or even exceeds) the first, with plenty of adventure that lasts to the end of the show. Then one day in the future, when we have become those older selves, we will look back and say, "Ah, I lived fully and well."

Pumpkin Tattoo

A Story

The sharp point of the big kitchen knife pierced the rind, opening the way for the blade to make its orbit about two inches from the stem of the pumpkin. Michael had told the kids pumpkin-carving would start after lunch, and here it was two o'clock. Nora and Jack would be back soon from their errands, and he would have nothing to show for his time alone with his grandkids other than sitting at the kitchen table reading the Sunday paper.

If Irene were here, she'd have them all crowded around her as she made cookies and listened to their exploits. He'd be there, too, the way he had on every trip to visit them. Now, more than ever, he realized that he'd been a satellite in so much of Irene's world. He ran his business and took care of the home repairs, but she did everything else. Now the job of grandparent was all his, and he had no idea what to do.

Michael plowed through the tangle of cleaning products under the sink looking for a large paper grocery bag. All he could find were the flimsy plastic ones.

The noise summoned six-year-old Jason, his hands empty of those game things he carried all day long. Michael scraped the pulpy underside of the pumpkin top carefully with the knife. "Guess I'm the only one who wants to make a jack-o'-lantern. Nobody showed up after lunch."

"But I do!" Jason cried.

"OK, take that big spoon and dig out the seeds inside the pumpkin. You can kneel on that stool over there." Michael pointed to a tall kitchen stool, which Jason then dragged over.

The clop-slap of shoes could only mean Cindy was on her way in the room, texting as she walked.

"We're carving the pumpkin!" Jason spattered seeds across the counter and onto the floor.

"Hand me a paper towel, will you?" Michael asked. The look his granddaughter gave him along with the paper towel could only mean one thing from a 13-year-old girl: Can't you see I'm busy? Michael let it pass. But if Nora had done something like that at thirteen . . . not that she would have sassed him. Nora had been his right-hand man on odd jobs since she was five.

"Where's John?" Michael asked.

Cindy shrugged. "Upstairs, maybe."

"Jason, go get him. Tell him we need his muscles." Jason ran out of the kitchen, yelling his brother's name.

Ten minutes later, John slouched against the wall, arms folded against his chest. "Pumpkins are for little kids."

"Fine, nobody needs you," Cindy told him.

Michael's head hurt from their squabbles and wished he could have sent them all out of the room. He thought of Irene, of what she might say or do. "You know, I met your grandmother over a pumpkin," he began.

Cindy's eyes were the first to meet his. "Really?"

"There was a community dance at the fire hall. It was October and the women's auxiliary had decorated the whole place with pumpkins and cornstalks. When I walked in, there was your grandmother at a table, helping her mother serve cider in these little glasses. I must have had fourteen glasses of cider that night just so I could see her. Finally, I got up enough nerve to ask her to dance."

The silence in the kitchen had a physical sensation to it as if the room had been stuffed with cotton. Cindy was the first to move, grasping him in a hug. "You miss her, don't you, Grandpa?"

"Every day." Michael wiped his eyes with a handkerchief from his back pocket.

The spoon clattered on the counter when John put it down. "So, let's make this one for her."

John made the first slice with the carving knife, and the face began to take shape: a nose with flared nostrils framed by eyes with a mischievous squint. With a flourish, he finished the mouth and stepped back to admire it. "Well, what do you think?"

"Very impressive," Michael said.

Cindy turned the pumpkin around to the back and picked up the carving knife.

"What are you doing" John shouted. "You're going to ruin it."

"No, I'm not," she replied calmly. This is just a small thing."

Michael reached out a long arm for the boy's shoulder; his hand landed gently. "Let's just see what she does."

At the top of the pumpkin, Cindy made a small, curved incision. The second curve closed the figure into the shape of a heart. "That's for us," she told him. "And Grandma Irene."

"Well, you didn't ruin it," John said, giving his sister a playful nudge.

Michael nodded, seeing in that tattoo a smile straight out of heaven. "I'd say it's just about perfect."

Nature Preserved

An Essay

A frozen path, crunching underfoot, leads from here to there: from the urban spaces of signs directing one-way traffic and painted lines for parking cars to nature's borderless stretch. Civilization gives up its grip slowly: a gate to manage the overly populated deer, shaggy in their winter-thickened hides; signs and pointing arrows; and a painted map with an "x" marking the spot of "you are here."

Yet, soon after this spoon-fed portal, nature spreads out her generous lap, covered with a winter quilt. This day, frigidly cold with a biting wind, nature does not hide her temperament; the harshness of elements pinch exposed ears and send gloved fingers up to a hat brim to tug it ever lower. The path, marked by hooves and boot treads, winds around the marshes—wetlands as delicate ecologically as spider's silk—where elements comingle: water, clear and motionless, now frozen crystalline solid; land, carpeted with stubbly marsh grasses and cattails, and lined with trees that extend skeletal reaches beyond the soil's limit; and sky, pale blue, drawing my eyes upward into an expanse so wide I have to be reminded it can be so. Nature preserved.

Home to creatures that inhabit all three elements, the preserve is meant to give them nest and rest, an oasis within a city. They exist within boundaries, fence lines that delineate the edges of their world, beyond which their existence would clash with unforgiving dangers. Nature protected, away from sprawl and (presumably) pollution; the way things were, the way things are supposed to be.

Yet another nature is preserved here. Like the deer and the ducks, I live within my boundaries; for me it is the 12x14 feet of my home office, with maroon walls tattooed with mementoes: the Navaho rug, the family portraits, the shelves of books. The space narrows further to the confines of a desk strewn with papers and notes, and constricts again to the cranial compartment of my writer's mind. But here, on a wooden bridge across the frozen marsh, I am released from my mental preoccupation, and I connect with memories, deep and powerful. On Cape Cod, one long-ago November day when my son was 3 and I pulled him in a red wagon along trails thick with oak and maple leaves. In upstate New York, I took a path marked only in my mind from the backyard of my childhood home, over a stone wall that once divided plots after the Revolutionary War, through the neighbor's meadow, and into my grandfather's woods. Countless nature hikes have led me through Wisconsin forests and over Hawaiian black sand.

I have forgotten neither these images nor the longing stirred every time for those places where earth and water and sky converge without a single human-made construct in the way. It's all there, in my wild little heart. Nature preserved.

Einstein's Theory of Love

A Story

The wave broke with a crackle against the small stones and bits of shell at the shoreline and a hiss of sea foam on the soft wet sand. The steady undulations of waves, where the Gulf of Mexico met the Florida coast, made Meghan wish she'd brought her camera to make a video for her sixth graders. Surely all of them had been to a beach somewhere, but to watch the waves—really watch them—was to observe nature's pulse.

Waves were everywhere, in water and in light. At the end of the school year, she'd do her final unit on "wacky science"—the quantum variety, boiled down to concepts for 11- and 12-year-olds, starting with her one-question pop quiz: "What is light made from—waves or particles?" Not having learned the lesson yet, the students could do little more than guess, usually a 40/60 split between the answers—and both were right.

Science was the reason Meghan became a teacher. Since she was a child, curiosity made her want to know such things as why waves break (when the height exceeds the water depth below the surface) and, later, Einstein's theory of the duality of light, sometimes particles and sometimes waves. It all depended to a large extent on what you were looking for. Meghan continued down the beach, feeling the warmth of those particles and waves on her SPF-50-coated skin. A 20-something man jogged barefoot, scattering shorebirds that rushed into the waves to gobble up a miniscule meal. An older couple strolled hand-in-hand, stooping now and then to examine a shell.

Watching them, Meghan thought of Gene, whom she'd been dating for three months. Had she asked him, he would have made the trip from Des Moines, Iowa, to Florida with her, but three months still seemed like such a short time. Besides, she knew the formula: *Wedding plus date equals disaster.* She'd proven that theorem a dozen years ago at a cousin's wedding when her date left her at the table, making it quite apparent that they were really "just friends."

Besides, Meghan argued with herself, it was so far to go for such a short trip—in Thursday night and out Sunday. Still, there were moments she regretted her decision, especially walking alone on this beach on Friday afternoon, two hours before the rehearsal. In the struggle between her practical nature and her romantic side, the logical part won out. But there was fear in that logic, she admitted. *If Gene had come, he would've met my friends, then when we split apart, there would be all that explaining to do . . .*

Meghan couldn't imagine being brave like her friend Jill, who at 34 was getting married for the first time to a man she'd met two years prior while on vacation along this very beach. Facing her 35th birthday in six months, Meghan had come to accept her own single status—and the wisdom of having made the trip by herself.

Meghan picked an arbitrary point up ahead to turn around. Just before she reached it, her phone buzzed in the pocket of her beach cover-up dress. She accepted the call without seeing the incoming number in the outdoor glare. "You on the beach?" Gene asked.

"How'd you guess?" she laughed.

Gene told her he wished he'd come, even if it were

only for a couple of days. "I know. I wish you had, too," she admitted.

Then he told her of the flight special he had found on the Internet. He could be there in plenty of time for the wedding on Saturday evening. Meghan smiled. It was a crazy idea and stupidly expensive . . . and all for only a day and a half together. And yet, she couldn't say no—not if she wanted to give the relationship a chance.

The practical part weighed in one more time, and there was no denying the logic of the reasoning. But the far larger part of her internal 40/60 split told her all that mattered was how she felt when Gene said he really wanted to come. Both answers were right, just like waves and particles. This time, though, she'd listen to her heart because, sometimes, being illogical made the most sense.

Lost Is Found

An Essay

Sitting at a coffee shop, deeply engrossed in conversation, I tucked a curl of hair behind one ear. As my fingertips brushed the lobe, it registered—empty. My hands flitted upwards, confirming an adorned right ear and a bare left.

I removed my scarf and shook it out, expanded my turtleneck, and then scanned the seat and the carpet below, but could not find my earring. Carefully retracing my steps, I returned to the counter where just twenty minutes earlier I'd ordered a decaf latte, and then walked to the door. Outside, a coating of snow had long since covered my footsteps. It was lost.

Material things do not last forever. They bend, break, go missing. But this earring was half of a precious pair with the delicate gleam of good gold—and a gift from my father who, while not exactly lost, had been gone for seven years that very month.

We lose any number of tangible things: hats, gloves, umbrellas. An entire anthology has been written on the fate of matchless socks and missing mates that enter the dryer only to be transported to some parallel universe. The intangible slip away just as easily: willpower, motivation, courage. "Abandon hope all who enter here," and we obey, all too often.

Where does it all go? I think of the black-fringed shawl I lost last summer and wonder if someone else is now wearing it; I hope so. I remember the lost-and-found table at my son's elementary school, many years ago, and the end-of-the-year notice that whatever was unclaimed would be donated. Lost today, repurposed tomorrow.

Or, think of the job that we feared would stymie our creativity, which became the start of someone else's dream career. Or the relationships we ran from—or that ran from us—because of poor timing or petty jealousies or any number of things, which became other people's twenty-plus-year marriages. And then there are 87-year-old fathers whose arteries clog and hearts give out. We collect losses like shells on the beach; by midlife, everyone has quite a pile.

And yet, there is the found. I remember one snowy day in upstate New York, decades ago, when my older sister, Jeannie, lost a beautiful sterling silver and enamel earring. The next July, as an eagle-eyed 8-year-old, I spied what I thought was a quarter, gleaming in the sun.

The jacket you swore you must have left at the movie theater was hanging on the coatrack at your friend's house all along. Dogs come home. Cats wander back. The estranged walk in the door.

Sometimes discovery comes by accident, but even then there is an element of purposefulness to it. Your friend was searching for her scarf when she found your jacket under the overcoat she seldom wears. I was on the lookout for pocket change when I saw Jeannie's earring in the grass. The loved one returns because the door, though shut, was not locked. Expectations keep the searchlight on.

To hope, however, is to leave open the possibility of disappointment and embarrassment over an outcome that's different than the one we long for. We have to risk being let down or appearing foolish. Not to do so, though, extinguishes possibility.

And so, I asked the woman behind the counter who had taken my money and frothed the milk for my drink if anyone had found a gold earring. She disappeared more deeply into the work area and asked a fellow server, who asked another, the echoes of their questions reverberating toward me. "Yes," I heard someone say from the kitchen. A key was produced, a drawer unlocked, and an earring deposited into the palm of my hand.

My father who gave me the earrings is still dead, but his love is still with me. Nothing is truly lost as long as there is hope.

Going to California

A Story

It was an old exodus, to move westward drawn by the promise of the new and the untested, to find or maybe lose oneself, as the case may be. At the moment, Jennifer Dresden thought of only one sojourner, her 20-year-old son, Jake, who could not be dissuaded from the notion that his destiny lay far west. He had "friends" in Los Angeles, fellow musicians he'd met online (but never in person) who had day jobs as messengers and behind the counter in pizzerias, who knew of gigs and people who were looking for talent. A guitarist, Jake had made up his mind: California was where he needed to be.

As a single mother, Jennifer had raised Jake with a sense of independence, so that he would never feel, directly or by implication, that he was responsible for her happiness. Now, as she folded yet another load of laundry, she wished she hadn't done such a good job.

His father hadn't been happy with Jake's plans to leave college as a sophomore. It was the one thing that had united the two of them, mother and father on the same page for once, until he caved in and Jennifer reluctantly gave her support.

"You don't have to do that, you know."

Jennifer leaned back to look out the doorway of the laundry room toward the kitchen where Jake stood in skinny jeans and a black t-shirt.

"Might as well start with clean stuff." Jennifer stuck her head far inside the dryer to see what was left behind.

"No, I mean I can't take much more. I've got two suitcases, my guitar, and a backpack. I'm going to borrow an amp, or buy one out there."

"I could always ship yours," Jennifer added. "Or maybe I'll bring it out with me when I come to visit." She silenced her too-helpful voice before she said more than she should and her suggestions hit the barrier of Jake's newly constructed boundaries. "Do you want breakfast?" she asked.

Jake pursed his lips. "We have any bacon?"

The microwave beeped and Jennifer checked the bacon strips, deciding they needed another 30 seconds. By the time it beeped again, Jake appeared in the kitchen, wearing a hooded gray sweatshirt.

"You should take your leather jacket. It gets cold in L.A. sometimes." Jennifer put a plate of eggs, bacon, and toast in front of him.

"I'll be fine, Mom. I won't do anything stupid. I'll get a job, and if it doesn't work out, I'll come back." He rattled the words and phrases off like a well-worked mantra, repeating the condensed version of conversations they'd had since his plan was first hatched. Jake quickly ate his bacon. Jennifer wanted him to slow down, knowing the quicker he ate, the closer he was to leaving.

Jennifer parked the car at the airport, against Jake's wishes and his protest that it was completely unnecessary, that it would be better to just drop and go. She waited while he checked his luggage and got his boarding pass and then walked him to the security line.

Jennifer leaned into the hug and held on for another moment, knowing it would have to last a long time, until she saw him again in California. Unless of course . . .

She stopped the thought, not wanting to imprint him with her silent hopes for failure and retreat.

"Don't give up on yourself," Jennifer announced into his shoulder. "Sometimes, these things take longer than you expect. If this is your dream, you have to go for it." She loosened her grip, but Jake tightened his. "Thanks, Mom. I know you believe in me."

"You bet I do!" Jennifer stepped back, forcing her hands into her pockets. "I know how talented you are. You've got to give this a shot. There is plenty of time in life for Plan B."

Jake sniffed and wiped his eyes once. "Maybe that's what we'll call it."

Jennifer cocked her head and gave him a lopsided grin. "What?"

"The band—Plan B."

As she exited the terminal and walked toward the parking garage, Jennifer imagined the liner notes or whatever they called them these days with digital music—the lyrics and musician credits, the bios of the performers, and a short mention of how the band had been named by the lead guitarist's mother in the airport. When he earned his Grammy, he might tell the story, or it would be their private joke as she sat in the front row of the theater and watched him perform. She imagined her daydreams and musings floating up into a cloud of possibilities, trailing behind her westbound son waiting for his flight, his future, and his fortune.

The Lost Wise Man

A Story

The boxes, wearing a thin layer of dust from a year's storage under the eaves, were brought down from the attic and stacked in the living room. The minute the cartons popped open and the folded-in flaps unfurled, there was only the wonder of treasure that had been buried since January to be unearthed during the shortest days of the year, as if the flash and sparkle could stave off the elongated night and the cold of a cynical world.

When Wesley and Jack, at 10 and 8, dove into the first box, their forearms disappearing up to the elbows, Hannah's only thought was of her sons as pirates, coveting doubloons from some Spanish galleon that was sent to the depths with all hands aboard. "Be careful, they'll break." Hannah repeated a refrain as traditional as the endless loop of "Frosty the Snowman" and "Jingle Bells" on the radio.

The decorations found their way to the usual places. The golden reindeer with a sprig of silk holly in its antlers always stood on the end table near the fireplace. A basket of cinnamon-scented pinecones and artificial branches, with red berries so real-looking a bird would have tried to feed on them, nestled in the corner of the hearth by the andirons.

"When your dad comes back from the store, we'll bring in the tree," Hannah told the boys, which sent them to the kitchen door to peer out at the garage as if her words could make him suddenly appear. She called to them: "Let's do the nativity while we wait." The little brown stable had been made by her Great-Great Uncle Hans, who gave it to his sister, Hannah's great-grandmother, as a wedding present in 1901. The real treasures, though, were the porcelain figures: a rosy-cheeked Mary with a blue veil slipping back from her forehead to reveal glossy brown hair; gentle bearded Joseph who crossed one hand over his heart and in the other held a staff; and two shepherd boys in short ragged pants, tunics, and vests. The donkey had lost an ear over the decades, and the cow's horns were chipped, but these small flaws were hardly noticeable. Two reclining sheep curled in opposite directions like a pair of parentheses. A blond angel hovered above, fastened to a pole over the stable with a wire loop on her back. The kings were majestically draped: Melchior in royal purple holding a domed-lid treasure box of gold; Caspar in emerald green with a matching turban, bearing frankincense; and Balthazar . . .

All activity ceased as boxes were emptied, examined, and then reexamined for the missing magi. Over and over, Hannah asked what could have happened to Balthazar? Surely he had been put away last Christmas.

That evening, with the tree in the corner sparkling with lights and decorations, Hannah scoured again.

"We can go out and buy another one," her husband, Dave, told her. "They sell these things everywhere,"

"You don't understand," Hannah wailed. "My great-grandmother gave it to my grandmother, my grandmother gave it to my mother, and my mother gave it to me."

"I know, I get it," Dave interrupted. "But we can't do anything about that now. So either we go with two kings or we find another set about the same size and bring in a new king."

For two days, Hannah shopped after work looking for

a suitable replacement, but could only find figures that were too big or too small. On the third day, when Hannah stooped to put water in the tree stand, she noticed an unfamiliar figure in the nativity, and something in pieces beside it.

Moving closer, she saw Balthazar, crumbled in four fragments rimmed with a milky plastic film that could only be a failed attempt to glue it back together. In his place, stood another figure, its proportions surprisingly right: Yoda in his Star Wars costume of brown tunic and matching cloak, bringing up the rear in the procession of the Three Kings.

One of the boys had done the damage, or perhaps they were both at fault in some way and complicity had kept them silent. The set was now ruined, incomplete, marred in its brokenness. And yet a stand-in was offered, by way of admission and apology, from two boys who knew they had to make it right the best way they could, while allowing for grace to fill in the gap.

Scooping up Balthazar's remains, Hannah tucked him into the palm of her hand, and moved Yoda a half inch forward to take his place among the magi.

Rewriting the Story of Your Life

An Essay

People tend to believe certain stories define their lives. For some, these are triumphant tales of overcoming odds or reaching a pinnacle of joy, happiness, and success. For most, however, the defining moments are more like an endless loop of unhappiness and disappointment, with a chiding moral of "that's the way life is." No matter how dire the details, these stories drag us down, causing us to believe that past performance is indicative of future returns.

When telling others the stories of our lives, repeating a sad, self-limiting story is like walking around with a permanent bad haircut, all the while pointing to your head and crying, "Look what happened to me!" The answer to changing this, however, is really quite simple: Rewrite your story. As a writer, I am talking about this quite literally. I have a whole repertoire of cry-in-your-cup-of-tea stories, from being bullied as a kid to recovering from bad relationships, as does everybody.

Consider the perils of my 7-year-old self: Jumping off the diving board into the community pool seemed like fun, except no one explained to me just how deep the water was—and I couldn't swim. Up the ladder I went, off the board I jumped, down into the water I sank. Popping up in a panic, I gulped and splashed, but nobody noticed. The lifeguard was asleep in the chair! My little friends tried to save me, but I dragged one girl down and she got out of the pool, fearing for her own safety. Just as I was about to give up, sure that I would drown, my arms started moving on their own accord, and I made it to the edge and pulled myself out. When my mother picked me up that afternoon, I tried to tell her what happened, but she told me to stop. That hadn't happened at all, she scolded. You made up the story.

Each time I've shared this story, I return to that sad little girl whose mother didn't believe what she said.

(In her defense, my mother was tired from a long day, and I seemed no worse for the wear.) Now, at midlife, I have to ask myself: Is this really a tale I want to keep telling?

We need to sort through the life stories we tell, pitching out the ones that no longer fit who we are and how we want to define ourselves. That's not to say we ignore our pasts or pretend things were different, but old stories can be reframed. What purpose does it serve if the tale you tell yourself makes you feel unlovable, unworthy, uncreative, unsuccessful, and un-everything else? If that's the story of your life that you've been telling yourself, what could you possibly believe about your future?

For me, the rewriting process begins by putting myself back into the scene I had envisioned so many times: the diving board, the pool, the plunge, the fear . . . Rather than skipping ahead to my mother's disbelief, I concentrate on the little girl in the white bathing suit with the blue-and-red trim. How did I feel when I pulled myself out of that pool, having been convinced just moments before that this was the end of my short life?

As I focus on that younger version of myself, I can literally feel how miraculous it had seemed. I took a risk, I nearly failed, but everything turned out okay in the end. How much better a tale is that to tell, particularly to myself, than the one I had been dragging around like a ratty old beach towel?

The new ending, just as true as the one I told before, draws from what I learned that day and what I believe to be true in my life: No matter how deep the water, I will save myself.

Now that's a story worth telling.

About the Author

Patricia Crisafulli, a former business journalist for Reuters, has authored several books on a variety of topics from leadership to women's issues, including the *New York Times* bestseller *The House of Dimon: How JPMorgan's Jamie Dimon Rose to the Top of the Financial World* (Wiley, 2009), and co-wrote two others, including *Rwanda, Inc.: How a Devastated Nation Become an Economic Model for the Developing World* (co-authored with Andrea Redmond, Palgrave Macmillan, 2012). Her first book was *Remembering Mother, Finding Myself: A Journey of Love and Self-Acceptance* (under the name Patricia Commins, HCI Books, 1999).

Patricia is the founder of www.FaithHopeandFiction.com, a free bi-monthly e-literary magazine that publishes original short stories, essays, and poetry. She is also a blogger on *Huffington Post,* writing on creativity and purpose.